IN ABSENTIA

Also by Morris Panych

Benevolence
The Dishwashers
Earshot
The Ends of the Earth
Girl in the Goldfish Bowl
Gordon
Lawrence & Holloman
Other Schools of Thought
7 Stories
Still Laughing
The Trespassers
Vigil
What Lies Before Us

All available from Talonbooks

IN ABSENTIA

MORRIS PANYCH

TALONBOOKS

Talonbooks
P.O. Box 2076, Vancouver, British Columbia V6B 3S3
www.talonbooks.com

Typeset in Cassia.
Printed and bound in Canada on 100% post-consumer recycled paper.
Cover design by Scott McKowen.

First printing: 2012

The publisher gratefully acknowledges the financial support of the Canada Council for the Arts, the Government of Canada through the Canada Book Fund, and the Province of British Columbia through the British Columbia Arts Council and the Book Publishing Tax Credit for our publishing activities.

Library and Archives Canada Cataloguing in Publication

Panych, Morris
    In Absentia / Morris Panych.

A play.
ISBN 978-0-88922-702-6

    I. Title.
PS8581.A65I5 2012   C812'.54   C2012-904180-7

In Absentia was first produced on January 31, 2012, at Montreal's Centaur Theatre with the following cast and creative team:

COLETTE	Jillian Fargey
EVELYN	Susan Glover
JASPER	Jade Hassouné
TOM	Paul Hopkins
BILL	Carlo Mestroni
Director	Roy Surette
Set and Costume Design	John C. Dinning
Lighting Design	Luc Prairie
Stage Manager	Melanie St-Jacques
Apprentice Stage Manager	Samantha Hogan
Assistant Director	Cameron Mackenzie

C A S T

COLETTE McKENNY, an attractive thirty-eight-year-old woman
JASPER, a young man
TOM McKENNY, Colette's husband
EVELYN, Colette's older sister
BILL, forty-something, a neighbour

S E T T I N G

The play takes place in the imagination – Colette's imagination, which includes memory, dreams, and hallucinations. In reality, the scenes happen in and around an upscale cottage on a lake, but naturalism should be kept to a minimum, as this will upset the dream-like, constantly drifting tone of the piece and take it out of its own milieu, which is the mind.

PRODUCTION NOTE

Characters and scenes will appear and disappear as trains of thought, like drifting snow on a lake; the piece is constantly in motion. Changes of tone or shifts in time or location are variously noted by a typographic ornament, a stage direction, or the arrival or departure of a character. In production this is accomplished largely through lighting changes and stage positions. There is simultaneous action throughout the play. The arrival and departure of characters should surprise us, but at the same time seem perfectly natural, as in a dream.

Tom, it should be noted, is visible only to Colette, and she often addresses him in the midst of dialogue with the other characters. Jasper, Evelyn, and Bill often remain onstage during the Colette and Tom sequences, but do not take part in them; instead, they go about their own business.

ACT ONE

Lights up on COLETTE and JASPER.
TOM stands at a distance.

TOM: You didn't come down to the tree today.

> *COLETTE chooses to ignore him. Instead, she speaks*
> *to JASPER, who is trying to warm up his hands.*

COLETTE: People love to swim out to that little island in the summer months. There's a pergola somebody built – I don't know who – covered over with trumpet vines. Apparently somebody owns the place, but nobody around here seems to know who it is. You can walk out there now on the ice.

JASPER: Not really an island, then.

COLETTE: Not if you can walk to it, no.

> *Beat.*

JASPER: I missed last winter entirely.

COLETTE: Well, I'm jealous.

JASPER: Stayed right out of the hemisphere.

COLETTE: I hate winter, especially this one.

JASPER: Yeah?

COLETTE: It's hard to believe anything will ever come
alive again.

JASPER: Then, suddenly, everything comes back.

COLETTE: Not always.

JASPER: I like the seasons; I missed them when I was away.

COLETTE: How are your fingers now?

JASPER: The blood's mostly come back.

COLETTE: I have terrible circulation, even in the summer.
When I go swimming, the blood goes right out of my fingers.
I look like a dead person. Mind you, I've never seen a dead
person –

JASPER: No?

COLETTE: No. But when I look down at my hands sometimes,
coming out of the water, I think, "Oh, this is what I'll look
like." My goodness, I'm talking a lot.

JASPER: Let me see your hands.

He takes her hands and turns them over.

I knew a girl who read palms for a living.

Beat.

COLETTE: Would you like some tea?

JASPER: Oh, I don't drink tea, Mrs. McKenny. It gives me a weird indigestion. Do you have any blueberry pie at all?

COLETTE: Uh – no.

JASPER: That's all right, then. When I was travelling, I always had a craving for blueberry pie.

> *Beat.*

It is funny what you miss the most.

COLETTE: It is.

JASPER: Like, you don't know who you are until you step out of your life for a bit.

COLETTE: How did you know my last name?

> *Beat.*

JASPER: It's on the mailbox outside?

> *Beat.*

Maybe I shouldn't have knocked at your door. This is – an imposition.

COLETTE: No, no. I'm glad you did.

JASPER: I'm glad I did, too.

COLETTE: I saw you out on the lake, and I thought, "My goodness, that poor young man," and I went out looking for you. I grabbed the parka and went out, but then I couldn't see you anywhere. I don't know what you were thinking, walking around in a jean jacket in this weather –

JASPER: I don't know what I was thinking. Sometimes you don't think.

COLETTE: Definitely the wrong hemisphere for that.

JASPER: It's only March; you forget what it's like.

COLETTE: How long have you been travelling?

JASPER: A while now. Quite a while now.

COLETTE: And you're on your way home.

JASPER: Yeah, well, "home" is a relative term.

COLETTE: Is it?

JASPER: I don't think anybody misses me, where I'm from.

COLETTE: They must.

JASPER: Is this your husband's parka?

COLETTE: Did I say I was married?

JASPER: No.

    Beat.

But this is not exactly a woman's coat.

COLETTE: It's my husband's, yes.

4

JASPER: And where is he?

COLETTE: Well, that's a bit of a story.

> *The lights begin to change a little. Her husband,*
> *TOM, appears.*

❄

TOM: Who's the kid?

COLETTE: I don't know. He was just standing there, out on
the lake.

TOM: Is he crazy?

COLETTE: Probably.

TOM: Is that why you didn't come down to the tree? I was
waiting for you.

COLETTE: Just appeared out of nowhere.

TOM: So you gave him my coat.

COLETTE: He was freezing to death.

TOM: Find out who he is.

COLETTE: What are you doing up here?

TOM: You don't want me here?

COLETTE: Don't tell me you're jealous.

TOM: No. A little.

COLETTE: Well, you can't be. And, anyway, I couldn't let him die of exposure.

TOM: Maybe I'm just looking out for you.

COLETTE: Because you think I can't look out for myself.

TOM: All right, maybe I'm looking out for me.

COLETTE: He's harmless.

TOM: Are you giving up on me?

COLETTE: How can you say that?

TOM: People forget; they move on with their life.

COLETTE: Life?

JASPER: What?

COLETTE: Sorry?

JASPER: Were you talking to me, Mrs. McKenny?

COLETTE: Yes, I was saying – what was I saying?

JASPER: You were going to tell me about your husband.

TOM: So tell him.

COLETTE: My husband is ... not here at the moment. He travels. For business.

JASPER: Right.

COLETTE: So –

Beat.

TOM: Awkward.

JASPER: May I use the facilities, ma'am?

TOM: Facilities?

COLETTE: (*to TOM*) It's a word.

JASPER: What?

COLETTE: Just down the hall.

JASPER goes.

TOM: You're lonely. I can't blame you for that.

COLETTE: It's twenty below; he would've frozen to death.

TOM: I suppose, in my absence –

COLETTE: You are so manipulative.

TOM: It's been a year now.

COLETTE: A year.

TOM: You can't just walk down to the tree every day and talk to nobody.

COLETTE: Yesterday I made a batch of oatmeal muffins and set them out for you.

TOM: You didn't burn them?

COLETTE: Maybe if I'm the perfect wife, you'll come back.

TOM: You still think our behaviour affects the outcome of things?

COLETTE: Yes, I burnt them.

> *TOM embraces her as she speaks; they rock slowly together, lost in their own world.*

And yes, I believe our behaviour affects the outcome.

TOM: Poor Colette.

COLETTE: You remember the old Greek woman, once, on that flight to wherever it was, dressed all in black, crossing herself, repeatedly?

TOM: Mrs. God-Help-the-Lot-of-Us?

COLETTE: Did you make that up or did I?

TOM: We thought it was so funny.

COLETTE: She prayed the whole trip.

TOM: And we landed safely, so thank you, Mrs. God-Help-the-Lot-of-Us.

COLETTE: We landed safely, exactly; so you couldn't exactly prove that her efforts were in vain.

TOM: Obviously they weren't.

COLETTE: Well, no, the plane would have to crash for that to happen, and then the secret would have died with us: prayers gone unanswered. We live in hope, Tom, not through evidence, but from lack of it.

TOM: That makes absolutely no sense.

COLETTE: I'm trying to be a good person, just in case.

TOM: You're not sleeping.

COLETTE: I'm afraid of my dreams. I drink too much; maybe I don't drink enough. I started a novel.

TOM: No comment.

COLETTE: "No comment" is a comment.

TOM: I retract.

COLETTE: I had to start something.

TOM: Are you sure it's a novel? You've only just started.

COLETTE: You have no faith in me.

TOM: Since we moved here, you haven't finished one thing.

COLETTE: I finished my poem.

TOM: Which one?

COLETTE: The endless one, the one I've been writing forever. I've finished it, for now. Anyway, can't you see how busy I am?

TOM: Inviting young men in from the cold.

COLETTE: Waiting for you is a lot of work. I mean, if I'm really going to focus on the job, do it up right. There's a lot of sighing involved and rereading that long novel by what's her name, and looking out the window, or trying not to look out the window. And I have my journal.

TOM: You don't have a journal.

COLETTE: That doesn't mean I won't start one.

TOM: Why don't you finish something?

COLETTE: Why don't you fuck off?

She didn't mean it.

Tom?

But TOM is gone. JASPER stands a little at a distance.

JASPER: Is this him?

JASPER is holding a framed photo.

COLETTE: What?

JASPER: Is this your husband?

COLETTE: No, that's a *picture* of him.

JASPER: Huh?

COLETTE: It's a joke; not a – very good one.

JASPER: I don't get it.

COLETTE: You asked if it was him. It's not really him, obviously; it's a –

She takes the photo from him.

My husband always, whenever I point to a picture of someone –

JASPER: Where is he?

COLETTE: What?

JASPER: Your husband? Where is he?

COLETTE: (*distantly*) As I say –

TOM: Where am I?

COLETTE: (*to TOM*) Usually the ice fisherman is out on the lake, but today he was gone. I see this kid, standing there –

JASPER: I used the soap beside the sink there; I hope that was appropriate.

COLETTE: (*to TOM*) – just looking up towards the house.

JASPER: This is rather a cool place.

COLETTE: Really? I just think of it as cold.

TOM: Just standing there?

COLETTE: (*to TOM*) I watched him for the longest time. He looked like you.

11

TOM: Him?

COLETTE: (*to TOM*) From a distance.

JASPER: You ever skate across this ice?

COLETTE: (*to TOM*) My heart almost jumped out of my chest
    as he walked towards me, more and more like you – as if you
    were returning from across the lake. I grabbed your parka;
    I ran out. I couldn't see him. I came back. For a moment,
    I thought I'd imagined the whole thing, then a knock at
    the door.

❄

*EVELYN appears, seated at a table. She chooses and
places letter tiles for a game of Scrabble.*

EVELYN: So, what, is he crazy, this kid?

COLETTE: How do you mean?

EVELYN: He has no coat?

COLETTE: He has a jacket. He's been away for a while.

EVELYN: Is that what they call it?

COLETTE: Call what?

EVELYN: Exactly. Where's he headed?

COLETTE: Thunder Bay, he says.

JASPER enters.

JASPER: Greetings!

COLETTE: This is Jasper, Evelyn.

EVELYN: Jasper?

JASPER: Like the town?

EVELYN: I've been there.

COLETTE: Evelyn is my older sister. She's been staying with me. She's been – what have you been doing, Evelyn?

EVELYN: This and that.

COLETTE: Everything.

JASPER: Cool.

EVELYN: Is it? Do you have to say "older sister"? I have other qualifications.

JASPER: I wouldn't have said "older," ma'am.

EVELYN: If you're trying to suck up to me, it won't work.

TOM: Evelyn.

COLETTE: (to TOM) Please.

TOM: Could there be a worse choice?

COLETTE: (to TOM) I'm beginning to believe she'll never go.

EVELYN: You don't mean that.

COLETTE: (*to TOM*) She keeps saying, "You don't mean that," as if she sincerely believes I don't mean it. She's been here six weeks; it feels like six months. The most depressing person in my family is here to cheer me up.

EVELYN: (*to JASPER*) This isn't exactly the way to Thunder Bay, you know.

JASPER: It is if you're in no hurry to get there.

EVELYN: Or anywhere.

> *Beat.*

> Well, look at the time.

JASPER: (*to COLETTE*) You were very kind to lend me the parka.

COLETTE: Keep it.

EVELYN: Really?

TOM: That's mine.

EVELYN: Isn't that one of Tom's?

TOM: (*to EVELYN*) Thank you.

JASPER: Thank you.

EVELYN: I'm going to get dinner started.

COLETTE: Would you like to stay for dinner, Jasper? Don't say no.

JASPER: Yes?

COLETTE: Yes, he says.

Beat.

EVELYN: Oh, good. I'll set an extra place.

JASPER: Let me help.

EVELYN and JASPER set the table.

COLETTE: (*to TOM*) She wants me to move on, but she doesn't want me to. She has swept in and filled the vacuum of my life. I get up in the morning, and the whole house is cleaner and neater than it ever was. The scent of bleach is everywhere, as if she's washing away all my unhappiness, or trying to. But as I keep telling her, there is nothing to mourn.

EVELYN: (*thinking COLETTE is speaking to her*) Let's hope not.

COLETTE: (*to TOM*) She's given up, you see. They've all given up on you, Tom. The police, the Department of External Affairs – even that annoying agent has stopped phoning here (the one who keeps trying to sell you that property next door). You know you're presumed dead when the real estate people stop calling.

JASPER gestures to another photo.

JASPER: Is this your honeymoon?

COLETTE: That was taken at Machu Picchu; it's the lost city of the Incas.

JASPER: I've been there.

COLETTE: Funny to say "lost." It was there all the time.

JASPER: Somebody found it all the same.

EVELYN: I made a rhubarb crumble.

JASPER: That's fine, ma'am. I don't mind rhubarb.

EVELYN: Oh, good.

COLETTE: (*to TOM*) Dear Evelyn – she's planted herself firmly in place. Like a big Boston fern you haven't got the heart to get rid of. She insists she doesn't want to be my sister; she wants to be my friend.

EVELYN: Leave the plates for me.

COLETTE: (*to TOM*) What is it you used to say?

TOM: A friend in need is a needy friend?

COLETTE: I don't want to be ungrateful.

TOM: Sure you do.

EVELYN: Let me do the dishes. You have enough on your mind.

JASPER: Yeah? Like what?

COLETTE: (*to TOM*) Funny, I have nothing on my mind at all.

EVELYN touches COLETTE's shoulder; COLETTE smiles sadly.

COLETTE: (*to TOM*) All the same, I have to show gratitude; I have to show gratitude mixed with a kind of dull sadness. I find myself playing the part of a grieving wife. It's exhausting.

BILL enters.

BILL: (*to COLETTE*) At least she means well.

COLETTE: (*to BILL*) As if that's all that matters.

BILL: It *is* all that matters. If everybody meant well, the world would be a better place.

COLETTE: (*to TOM*) Evelyn isn't bad enough, I have Bill hanging around all the time now –

EVELYN: (*to BILL*) Look who's here!

COLETTE: (*to TOM*) – engaging me in earnest conversation.

TOM: What can you say about Bill?

BILL: Don't you want the world to be a better place?

COLETTE: (*to BILL*) Of course I do. (*to TOM*) I don't, really, but then we'd have to talk about it.

EVELYN: (*to BILL*) Could you have a look at the vacuum cleaner when you get a minute?

BILL: Sure.

BILL and EVELYN exit.

TOM: Good old reliable Bill.

COLETTE: (*to TOM*) It's that belief – that confidence – that anything can be fixed. Where does he get that confidence? Where does he get that sense of never doubting?

TOM: Maybe he's just overcompensating for the rest of us.

BILL re-enters with EVELYN.

BILL: If I can't get the part for it this week, I'll just rebuild the motor.

COLETTE: (*to TOM*) The man can rebuild a car, and I can hardly even drive one.

JASPER reappears for a moment.

JASPER: Should I be going now, Mrs. McKenny?

COLETTE: Colette.

JASPER: Colette.

EVELYN: So soon?

BILL: I can take you into town.

COLETTE: There's no hurry.

EVELYN: No?

JASPER: Let me help out with the dishes.

JASPER goes to the kitchen.

EVELYN: He's helping out with the dishes.

A loud crash sounds offstage.

JASPER: (*offstage*) Sorry!

BILL: Where's he staying, I wonder?

COLETTE: How should I know?

BILL: All the motels are closed.

COLETTE: Maybe he should stay here.

Beat.

BILL: Right. I was going to say.

EVELYN: That's very hospitable of us.

COLETTE: Up until now, it was just me, Bill, Evelyn; imagine the fun.

EVELYN: I'm going to set up the Scrabble game.

She chooses and places word tiles under the following action.

❄

COLETTE: (*to TOM*) She has this terrible crush on Bill.

TOM: Really?

COLETTE: Men never notice anything.

TOM: Until they're not here anymore.

COLETTE: She's had it for years. He just finds her annoying.

BILL: No, I don't.

COLETTE: Yes, you do.

BILL: I do.

COLETTE: Why are you so dishonest with her?

BILL: How am I dishonest?

COLETTE: You flirt with her.

BILL: That's got to be by accident.

COLETTE: Why are men always nicer to the women they pity than the women they actually like?

BILL: I'm polite.

COLETTE: Politeness, as we all know, is the sincerest form of dishonesty.

TOM: Nicely said.

COLETTE: Thank you.

EVELYN: (*to BILL*) Right.

COLETTE: (*to TOM*) There's nothing I enjoy more than leaving those two alone in a room together.

> *JASPER enters from the kitchen.*

JASPER: All done.

COLETTE: Jasper and I are going for a walk.

EVELYN: But I picked your letters for you.

COLETTE: Bill can play them.

EVELYN: Bill can play them.

COLETTE: (*to TOM*) As long as he comes around, she's happy. But, God, she makes the most tragic Freudian slips.

EVELYN: I bet you've got a great big word.

BILL: Is *Q-R-N-X-V-Y-L* the correct spelling for "qrnxvyl"?

EVELYN: Terrible letters are like life. You finally get a *Q* but then the *U* never shows up.

BILL: Meaning?

COLETTE: (*to TOM*) Evelyn should never be cryptic.

EVELYN: You can trade all your letters in and miss a turn, but then you're missing a turn, which is –

BILL: What have you done to your hair?

EVELYN: Combed it.

BILL: Oh?

❄

COLETTE: (*whispering to EVELYN*) Bill is an organic farmer, Evelyn, not a nineteenth-century English vicar. You should wear some lipstick.

EVELYN: What's Bill got to do with anything? Bill is attracted to you.

COLETTE: Bill just needs to get laid.

EVELYN: You think that's all it is?

COLETTE: He's a man, isn't he?

EVELYN: And, anyway, can't a person rethink their appearance?

COLETTE: (*louder*) In the middle of nowhere?

❄

BILL: (*appearing*) This is hardly the middle of nowhere.

COLETTE: Oh, Bill, you're always so positive. Positive Bill.

BILL: You want us to be.

COLETTE: Do I?

BILL: You said, I think you said, something about not being despondent.

COLETTE: Because you have no reason.

BILL: We're in this together. We all want Tom back.

COLETTE: (*to TOM*) See? We all want you back, Tom. We're all in this together.

TOM: Terrific.

BILL: I'm just trying to understand your pain.

COLETTE: (to TOM) Why does anybody ever want to try and understand anybody else's pain? We run screaming from our own; why are we so attracted to other people's?

TOM: He's a heck of a nice guy.

COLETTE: Don't say that; I know exactly what you're trying to do. I don't need a nice guy; if I'd needed a nice guy, Tom, I wouldn't have married you.

TOM: Sweet.

COLETTE: I'm not attracted to him.

TOM: I don't mind if you are.

COLETTE: Good. I was. I wanted to sleep with him.

TOM: Oh.

COLETTE: Last year. I had it planned. Not completely planned, but somewhat mapped out.

TOM: And now?

COLETTE: Now it's the furthest thing from my mind. I feel dirty around him. I feel as if my attraction to him precipitated this whole thing.

TOM: Oh, here we go again.

COLETTE: Events are connected.

TOM: So your romantic feelings towards your neighbour, the organic farmer, caused me to be abducted by leftists.

COLETTE: I haven't quite connected all the dots.

TOM: That's a lot of dots.

COLETTE: And now this kid appears; you see?

TOM: Right.

❄

JASPER: You play guitar?

COLETTE: It's my husband's; he doesn't play.

TOM: Correction – I don't play *well*.

COLETTE: (*to TOM*) And I hardly need any criticism from you.

TOM: I'm observing. Can't I observe?

COLETTE: Yes, you observe from that distance of yours, that critical distance. You've never participated in my life, not in any real way. Whenever I get excited about something, whenever I feel something – really feel something –

TOM: Colette; I'm an engineer.

❄

COLETTE is becoming tipsy.

COLETTE: (*to TOM, slurring her words*) The second he appeared I sensed that things could change, untie this ... knot that we've all tied ourselves into. Inject a little life into this long year of winter.

TOM: Maybe you should ease up on the booze.

COLETTE: (*to TOM*) Maybe you should go fuck yourself.

COLETTE continues in her giddy drunkenness, accompanied by JASPER.

JASPER: Watch it, Mrs. McKenny.

COLETTE: You have to call me by my first name. I told you.

EVELYN appears.

EVELYN: What is this?

COLETTE: Just us.

EVELYN: We were so worried. Where were you?

COLETTE: The bar. Who won the Scrabble game?

EVELYN: You drove into town?

COLETTE: Jasper drove. I'm a terrible driver.

JASPER: She's quite the dancer, though.

EVELYN: I didn't know there was dancing at O'Grady's.

COLETTE: There is now.

JASPER: She has natural talent.

EVELYN: Does she.

COLETTE: Don't worry about Evelyn. Evelyn is here to help me, so she gets overly concerned about – what is it you always get so overly concerned about?

JASPER: She's here to help you what?

COLETTE: She cheers me up. Isn't that funny?

JASPER: You seem pretty cheery to me.

COLETTE: Oh, but I'm not. I'm miserable. And Evelyn is helping me; aren't you, Evelyn?

EVELYN: You've had a bit to drink.

JASPER: She's had a lot to drink.

COLETTE: We're exercising patience, here. We're waiting out the pain, Jasper. Playing Scrabble – isn't that right, Evelyn? – putting our focus into things we can – actually piece together. And if we don't like our predicament, well, we can just trade in our letters and start over.

JASPER: I don't get you.

EVELYN: Her husband is missing.

JASPER: Like, how?

COLETTE: Not *missing*, just somewhere we don't know about. Lost.

EVELYN: He was kidnapped.

JASPER: Really?

EVELYN: By – people who wanted money. But then they didn't
    want the money anymore. They just – disappeared. Thank
    you for bringing her back.

JASPER: She threw her shoe out the car window.

COLETTE: Do we have any tequila?

EVELYN: No.

COLETTE: We need to get that. Can I offer you some white
    wine? It's all we have, I'm afraid. Evelyn doesn't like me to
    keep real alcohol in the house in case I might decide to drink
    it. Evelyn is a dear, dear older sister, you know; I'm sorry, not
    older – earlier. She cares about me, you know. Ever since we
    were – she does. She cares. Evelyn, you care about me, don't
    you. Evelyn is a nurse. She knows how to look after people
    she doesn't care anything about, but, no, she cares about me
    because I'm family and she has to.

JASPER: Where did they go?

COLETTE: Huh?

JASPER: The people who kidnapped your husband. Where did
    they go?

COLETTE: We lost contact. Isn't that right, Evelyn. We were
    emailing them. Isn't that funny? Maybe we should have put
    in a few more of those little sideways happy faces. Emoticons,
    is that it? *E-mo-ti-cons*. Look: sad, happy, sad. Would you care
    for some ice cream? Do we have ice cream, Evelyn? We

usually have ice cream. After all, I can't kill myself with ice cream – however much I'd like to try.

EVELYN: I don't think he wants ice cream.

JASPER: What flavour?

> *JASPER and COLETTE laugh, like those people who share a hilarious joke nobody else gets.*

❄

BILL: So he stayed the night?

EVELYN: Upstairs, on his roll-up.

BILL: She's free to do what she wants.

EVELYN: She doesn't know what she wants. She talks to him, you know. She stands behind a tree down by the dock; she thinks I can't see her. She talks to Tom.

BILL: She's lonely.

EVELYN: She's more than lonely. She's amputated.

BILL: She what?

EVELYN: People who lose a limb; they think the limb is still there.

BILL: Wow, that's –

EVELYN: Yeah.

BILL: What kind of a name is "Jasper"?

EVELYN: He carries a backpack.

BILL: What's in it, I wonder.

EVELYN: Don't ask me. Almost nothing.

BILL: Which tree?

❅

COLETTE: I woke up this morning, honestly expecting some
kind of crack in the ice. That sound, that sound under the ice
is getting louder, like something pounding to get out, but I
think the days are actually getting colder. How can it go on
for so long? I'm losing my faith. There isn't a bird in the sky.
There isn't a person on any road. The checkout woman at the
Handy Mart said to me yesterday, "I never take spring for
granted." What if that were true, Tom? What if this time it
didn't happen? What if we went through March and April
and May and June and all through the summer and into the
fall and right back into winter again, and nothing came to
life, nothing flowered, nothing opened itself and created
anew; what then? Then none of us would ever take spring for
granted again. And we would wait, we would wait –
breathless – for the first sign of hope. And tears would well
up in our eyes, yearning for a second chance. And we would
say, "If you come, if you come back this time, we will forever,
forever, believe in you, and never, ever take you for granted."

TOM: You think you took me for granted?

COLETTE: Is that what I said? I don't even know what I'm
saying anymore.

TOM: How, exactly?

COLETTE: I wasn't a *wife* in that way that some women are; I never made a household for you the way someone like Evelyn can. She preserves pears; can you believe it? I can't even preserve my dignity.

TOM: I like you the way you are.

COLETTE: No, you don't, and, anyway, you're only saying it because I'm imagining you are. You never liked me the way I was. You were always trying to change me. And when you couldn't change me, you humoured me, or ignored me.

TOM: I think that's called a relationship.

COLETTE: I'm selling your golf clubs, by the way.

TOM: Ah.

COLETTE: They remind me of something about you I never liked.

TOM: What?

COLETTE: The scorecard. You knew I couldn't play, but you jotted down my score, anyway.

TOM: I never added it up, if it makes you feel any better.

COLETTE: I put up little notices in town. I'm sure people think I've given up hope. "Oh, look, she's selling his golf clubs; that's it, then." I've got the grocery-store manager flirting with me already.

TOM: You're punishing me in some way.

COLETTE: Why not? There are times, to tell you the truth, I think you faked this whole thing.

TOM: It's a pretty elaborate ruse. Hiring a gang of fake kidnappers. Beating myself up, sending you a picture.

COLETTE: You're a pretty elaborate guy.

TOM: And to what end?

COLETTE: To – I don't know – reinvent yourself? Have you never wanted to reinvent yourself?

TOM: Was I not happy with my life?

COLETTE: Why did you always travel?

TOM: For work?

COLETTE: Lots of people work; they get up in the morning, they go downtown, not down to South America.

❆

JASPER appears.

JASPER: What?

COLETTE: Sorry?

JASPER: South America?

COLETTE: Yes.

JASPER: And they sent you a picture of him, all beat up? That's –

COLETTE: You sure you don't want some toast?

JASPER: I don't eat in the morning.

COLETTE: No? Why is that?

JASPER: I like hunger. I like the feeling of it in my stomach.

COLETTE: What is it about the feeling in your stomach you like?

JASPER: Emptiness.

> *Beat.*

Here. I brought you this.

> *JASPER pulls a little Madonna figurine from his pack and hands it to COLETTE.*

COLETTE: Thank you.

> *She studies it.*

What do you mean, you brought me this?

JASPER: Huh?

COLETTE: You said you brought me this.

JASPER: From my travels.

COLETTE: But you didn't know me on your travels.

JASPER: Maybe I did.

Beat.

JASPER: You know how you can know somebody before you ever meet them?

TOM: Huh?

COLETTE: (*to TOM*) I think I know what he means.

TOM: I don't.

COLETTE: (*to JASPER*) It's a Virgin Mary.

JASPER: Is that what it is?

She studies the statuette, then him.

COLETTE: I wonder why you're here.

JASPER: Huh?

COLETTE: I believe there's a reason for things. I was wondering what the reason for you was.

JASPER: Hey. The reason is the reason.

COLETTE: What do you believe in?

JASPER: I believe in the number six.

COLETTE: Oh, that's good. So you do believe in something. You believe in the number six.

JASPER: It's a good number. I always bet six.

EVELYN appears.

EVELYN: How did you come up with that number, in particular?

JASPER: Trial and error. Everybody has a number.

COLETTE: What's mine?

JASPER: I don't know. But everybody has one.

COLETTE: You think so?

JASPER: It wouldn't be fair if some people had a number and other people didn't. Everybody has a number; you just need to find it.

COLETTE: (*to TOM*) Where do we find it? Where do we find this number? Who hands it out, I wonder. He doesn't believe in God, this kid, but he believes in tarot cards and aliens and numbers.

❄

BILL: I think your number is one.

COLETTE: Do you?

BILL: Or – two.

COLETTE: You said "one" first. Why did you say "one"?

BILL: Your – singularity.

COLETTE: Oh, Bill, you're so transparent sometimes.

BILL: Banal is what I think you mean.

COLETTE: I think your number is *two*. As in too much, as in too soon, and yet somehow too late. (*in response to his reaction*) Too sweet. You're too sweet, is what I meant.

BILL: I think my number *is* two.

COLETTE: Yes, but my number is one, so – that doesn't really work out, does it?

BILL: I shouldn't have said that.

COLETTE: No, you should have said that. We need to make our intentions known.

BILL: This isn't the right time.

COLETTE: When would be the right time?

BILL: You need to come full circle with this.

COLETTE pauses, trying not to lose control.

COLETTE: You can't say "full circle." That implies a continuum. There's no continuum here. There's no "getting over" and "moving on." Understand? There's no "this has changed my life in so many unexpected ways and made me a stronger person."

BILL: Sure.

COLETTE: There's no new beginning. Sorry.

BILL: No.

BILL exits.

COLETTE: (*to TOM*) Poor Bill. I used to have a real thing for him. It might have been more than a thing. When life was – back then – when life was you going away for three months, and me staying up here at the cottage and trying to write, and Bill was chopping the wood and fixing the hot-water tank – I had a thing for him. And last time, just before you left, one night, lying in bed, I took it into my head that I might just sleep with him when you were gone.

TOM: But you didn't.

COLETTE: It doesn't matter. I was going to.

TOM: You don't know that.

COLETTE: I would have. You think I can't do things. I would have slept with him. A couple of times, before we got the first communication, a couple of times that very week, I got myself all bathed and done up and had him over for dinner. The first time, he didn't respond to my obvious, shameless advances. Probably because he's just so pathologically decent. The second time, we came very close. There would have been a third time. But then, that very evening, we got the first communication. After that, everything changed. I don't have any feelings for him now, at all. Oh, I have feelings, but not those feelings. There was a time when Bill brought me to life. Well, not life, being Bill, but – semi-consciousness. That time is gone.

TOM: So it's the kid now.

COLETTE: Oh, for fuck's sake, Tom, it's not the same thing. He symbolizes something for me. How can you not get that? This morning I woke up, I got out of bed, and I threw open

the drapes. Evelyn always opens them; this morning, I did it.
I threw them wide open to let the sun in. Finally.

TOM: There was a blizzard.

COLETTE: You get the idea.

❄

JASPER: Maybe I should think about going.

COLETTE: Not in this weather. You can't.

❄

EVELYN: How long is he staying, then?

COLETTE: How long is anybody staying?

EVELYN: If you're trying to be hurtful, you're not succeeding. I
know you don't mean what you say half the time.

COLETTE: It's only a question, Evelyn. Nobody is asking you to
leave, so why should we ask him to?

EVELYN: I'm your sister.

COLETTE: And he's my friend.

EVELYN: You met him three days ago. He came out of nowhere.

COLETTE: Not out of nowhere, Evelyn. He was waving to me
out there.

EVELYN: What?

COLETTE: When I first saw him out there on the lake, he was looking back at me, and he was waving.

EVELYN: Why?

COLETTE: It's like he knows me.

EVELYN: Oh, Colette.

COLETTE: All right, I'm crazy.

EVELYN: And I'm not impressed with his candour.

COLETTE: By that you mean walking around in his underwear?

JASPER enters with a guitar, wearing only his underwear; he strikes a chord.

JASPER: Woah. This needs some tuning.

COLETTE: (*to EVELYN*) Besides, he has interesting things to say, on all kinds of subjects. Not strictly true, but in his defence he's pretty cute, and he does come out with some awfully sweet notions.

JASPER: (*tuning the guitar*) It's not a sweet notion; it's a whole philosophy, man.

COLETTE: All right, a whole philosophy.

JASPER: Everybody knows the world isn't flat; the world isn't flat – that's not what I'm saying.

COLETTE: What are you saying?

JASPER: It's a mental –

COLETTE: Construct.

JASPER: A perception thing. If the earth is round, why don't we see it that way?

COLETTE: We take it on faith.

JASPER: But don't you trust your perception more?

He strums.

EVELYN: So why isn't it cold everywhere, for instance?

JASPER: Huh?

EVELYN: There's a blizzard outside; why isn't there a blizzard in Hawaii?

JASPER: There might be; we're not there.

EVELYN: The earth is round, sorry.

JASPER: Because somebody told you it was.

COLETTE: You see, Evelyn, because somebody told you it was.

EVELYN: Would you like a pair of pants?

JASPER: Why don't you respect me?

EVELYN: What?

COLETTE: Don't you respect him, Evelyn?

EVELYN: I never said that. I never said I didn't – respect him.

JASPER: Do you respect me?

EVELYN: Respect you?

COLETTE: Evelyn – is not always good with people; she works in health care.

EVELYN: I'm not good with half-naked people who think the earth is flat.

COLETTE: I am.

JASPER: Our thoughts are more real than our actions –

EVELYN: Where'd you find that, in a hookah pipe?

JASPER: Reality is fluid, man; like water can change to ice and back again – like the lake. The lake is solid, and soon it won't be. What's that about?

EVELYN: You want reality? Work in the dialysis unit.

COLETTE: At least, Jasper, you admit what most men only dare to think.

JASPER: What about your husband?

COLETTE: What about him?

JASPER: What did he believe?

COLETTE: He definitely believes the world is round; my God, he goes around and around it enough.

JASPER: You talk about him like he's still alive.

COLETTE: He is still alive.

JASPER: That's not what I'm thinking.

COLETTE is taken aback.

COLETTE: What?

JASPER: What?

EVELYN: Scrabble, anyone? Here. Pick your letters.

❄

BILL: He's a dumb kid.

COLETTE: *(to BILL)* Why would he say it?

BILL: He's an idiot. Did I say that already? He's an idiot.

COLETTE: I don't think he's an idiot.

BILL: What's he still doing here?

COLETTE: He's sort of a drifter.

BILL: So why doesn't he keep drifting?

❄

JASPER: I have a mission, Bill.

BILL: And what's that?

JASPER: I can't talk about it, okay? I want to change people. I want to – make things better.

BILL: I thought you couldn't talk about it.

JASPER: The details.

BILL: Who set you on this mission?

JASPER: Nobody. Somebody. Inside me, I felt it.

BILL: Change people how?

JASPER: I'm kind of making it up as I go along.

BILL: And how are you changing me?

JASPER: It's like air currents, man. It's like – the tide.

BILL: Oh, you're right. I feel changed already.

❄

COLETTE: (*to TOM*) But he is changing things. He's bringing the sun back; slowly it's starting to slant its way over the deck. There are slivers of light fingering their way up the walls.

TOM: When spring comes, it's the end of waiting, you know.

COLETTE: The end of waiting.

TOM: But winter is only holding everything frozen, in place. What you wait for – what happens when it does come? If spring returns and I still don't?

❄

JASPER: I believe his love will find a way back to you.

COLETTE: Will it?

JASPER: I don't know. I don't know.

❄

COLETTE: (*to TOM*) You promised as much. Before you went, you said, "I'll be back in no time," and then you left again, but like an idiot I believed you. I always believed in you, even when I knew you were lying –

TOM: Lying?

COLETTE: Or not telling me everything.

❄

EVELYN: It's not true.

COLETTE: It is.

EVELYN: Tom. How do you know?

COLETTE: I know.

EVELYN: You've always had an overactive imagination.

COLETTE: It was his credit-card statement. There was an item from last January. When he was in San Francisco. Mini-bar tab. It isn't actually itemized, but I know he never uses the mini-bar because he's too cheap, so I called the hotel, thinking there was mistake. No. A liqueur: Baileys Irish Cream. Well, I know he doesn't drink that. It's really why I called the hotel, to confirm what I already knew.

EVELYN: Could have been a colleague.

❄

TOM: Could have been.

COLETTE: Could have been, yes. Which is why, that night, when you were back, Tom, in that restaurant, after dinner, I ordered the Baileys. You looked at me.

TOM: That's right.

COLETTE: We both knew. And you sat there, with that bemused expression. I knew, and you knew I knew. But we let it slide. I love you, Tom. That's all that matters now. People have affairs. It happens. If you would come back, I wouldn't care about anything. And yet, the night before you left, I wanted you to leave. Couldn't wait for you to get out of the house. Bill was over for dinner the very next night, and two more nights after that.

❄

BILL appears wearing an old suit.

BILL: Is this all right?

COLETTE: He showed up in a suit the last time – I think it was about thirty years old. (*to BILL*) You look so handsome.

BILL: It's – been a while.

Beat.

What are we doing?

COLETTE: Having dinner. (*to TOM*) I knew what he was thinking. You can see right through Bill.

BILL: Having dinner, right. We're having dinner.

COLETTE: (*to TOM*) I wasn't exactly making a secret of my intentions, either. Still, we did nothing. I think both of us were waiting for the other person to make the next move, as if that would spare us from absolute guilt. We could say we just – fell into the thing. Or almost. (*to BILL*) How's your wine?

BILL: How's yours?

> *They get close. The computer sounds with an email alert, and the spell is broken.*

I think it's your email.

COLETTE: That'll be Tom.

BILL: Funny how far away a person can be and still be in the room.

COLETTE: What are we doing in that part of the world, anyway? What are we doing in bloody Tumaco, Colombia?

BILL: *I'm* not there.

COLETTE: We're all there. Our fingers in every little thing.

BILL: Some sort of oil pipeline, isn't it?

COLETTE: Whose oil? Not ours.

BILL: Hey. It's business.

COLETTE: And what are we offering in return?

BILL: Less than it's worth probably; that's business. Do you really want to have this conversation?

COLETTE: No.

BILL: I don't really know what we're doing there. I just assume it's something that's helping those people almost as much as it's helping us.

COLETTE: What if it isn't?

BILL: Is that a new dress?

COLETTE: (*to TOM*) Do you remember, Tom, our second anniversary? We decided we were going to have a baby? I got all sexy. I wore that dress. And how long did that dream stay alive in our minds? For so long it identified us. For so long it made us not whole. Even now, looking out over the landscape, trees stripped of their meaning, I still feel as if it defines us. Empty. Jasper says he likes the feeling of emptiness. I know that feeling. I know hunger. I wanted a baby. Not for me, for you.

❄

JASPER: I like trees without their leaves.

COLETTE: You do?

JASPER: It's like the sad truth nature is telling us: things come and things go.

COLETTE: You're right. They're beautiful in their nakedness.

*

BILL: So are you having sex with him?

COLETTE: I don't know. Is yoga sex? I suppose, for me, at this
point –

*

JASPER takes a yoga position: the tree pose.

JASPER: It comes from India.

COLETTE: Apparently it comes from India.

BILL: He gets around.

JASPER: India is beautiful, man. Beautiful. Reincarnation;
all that.

EVELYN: And malaria and dengue fever and tetanus.

COLETTE: I've never been there.

JASPER: Yeah.

> *Beat.*

Me neither.

COLETTE: No?

JASPER: But I've been to Central America, Peru; I've been to
Colombia.

COLETTE startles.

JASPER: What did I say?

EVELYN: It's where Tom disappeared.

❄

COLETTE: (*to TOM*) Do you believe in synchronicity, Tom?

TOM: I'll say no.

COLETTE: Not even a little bit?

TOM: Sometimes things don't make sense, Colette. Sometimes a
random event is just a random event.

COLETTE: Spoken like a true scientist.

TOM: I'm not a true scientist. I work for an oil company.

COLETTE: Your abduction was not a random event.

TOM: Well, there's an equation if you want one. Wrong place
plus wrong man, over right time.

COLETTE: The woman on the plane; the old Greek woman –
she kept the plane in the air.

TOM: The air kept the plane in the air.

COLETTE: But somebody, somewhere, is doing something. Or
not doing something. Everything is connected. People don't
just – disappear. There is wrong in the world, and the wrong
is being redressed.

TOM: Maybe this is part of your process of grieving.

COLETTE: I'm not grieving. It's not a process.

TOM: It's an onion, right? Peeled back, layer after layer.

COLETTE: An onion.

TOM: Layer after layer.

COLETTE: What have you been reading?

TOM: It's you that's been reading it. I'm just reminding you.
Different thoughts, different rationales enter your head. It's
necessary. You need to make sense of something that makes
no sense. You need to assign blame.

COLETTE: I stopped reading that stupid book.

TOM: There's no order to any of it. It simply unfolds.

COLETTE: I've never done anything good in my life, and this is
my punishment.

TOM: How did I deserve to be abducted any more than, say,
three hundred other people in that marketplace on that
particular day?

COLETTE: I don't know. Because you were cheating on me.
Because I wanted to pay you back. I wished it.

TOM: You wished me to be kidnapped and tortured?

COLETTE: I wished you to go away.

TOM: And now you wish I would come back.

COLETTE: Every time you left, I would say a little prayer that you would return to me safely. This last time, I didn't. I don't know if I forgot or if it was on purpose –

TOM: You said you've never done anything good in your life –

COLETTE: I haven't. I have not made one single positive contribution to the betterment of humanity, with the noble exception of the compost heap.

❄

BILL: You let Evelyn stay, even though she's driving you crazy.

COLETTE: I'm just too much of a coward to say, "Go." Besides, in some ways it's good to have her around. It does me good to test my patience every single day by not killing her. Look how well I'm doing: Evelyn, still not dead.

EVELYN: You don't mean that.

COLETTE: Of course not. (*to TOM*) I do mean that, but what good does it do to say it? She doesn't accept my true feelings, so I have to invent fake ones. She thinks I should be crying when we watch a sad movie, so I pretend to cry, so she can cry.

EVELYN: Let it out.

❄

COLETTE: (*to TOM*) She thinks in this way that I will come to purge myself of sadness. She doesn't understand. Sadness is an affectation compared to this. This isn't feeling. This is the absence of all feeling. There is nothing inside me. This is winter inside. It's not like I have some well of tears to be emptied. There are no tears; there is no well. I understand why Jasper likes the feeling of hunger. At least it's something that moves you; drives you forward.

TOM: So he's your one good thing. So you're trying to redeem yourself through him.

COLETTE: Redeem myself?

TOM: You take him in, you look after him for a while. The kind act may be rewarded.

COLETTE: How?

TOM: Well, you seem to be assigning a kind of moral commodity to your behaviour –

COLETTE: Taking in Jasper – I don't know how good that is.

❄

JASPER: I have places to go.

COLETTE: (*to TOM*) He has places to go. (*to JASPER*) What places?

JASPER: Places. I didn't mean to stay this long.

COLETTE: Tell me about the places you've been. Tell me about Colombia.

JASPER: I was with a girl I met in Cancun. We went to Cartagena. She ran into some Americans, and they took off together, back to Mexico, I think.

COLETTE: Were you in love with her?

JASPER: No. Yes.

COLETTE: Was she pretty?

JASPER: I don't remember. Why do you need to know this?

COLETTE: I don't need to know it.

JASPER: I don't remember her face. I remember she had a –
a tattoo on her hand, a hummingbird.

COLETTE: Really?

JASPER: I think she was a drug smuggler. She always lied to me.
But I pretended to believe her, just to see where it would go. I
think she was Dutch. I'm pretty sure she was Dutch.

COLETTE: What were you doing in Cancun?

JASPER: I don't know.

❅

BILL: How can he not know?

COLETTE: Well, it's Mexico; what's to know? He's a kid; kids
drift. Didn't you drift?

BILL: Sure.

COLETTE: Oh, Bill, you're just saying that. I bet you're the only
person in the world who's always known exactly what he
wants.

BILL: I know what I want now.

EVELYN: What are you afraid of with Bill? A little companionship?

COLETTE: It's more than companionship.

EVELYN: It's been a year. It's been a year, Colette, since anybody's heard.

COLETTE: No, it hasn't.

TOM: It has, actually.

BILL: Nobody's rushing you.

COLETTE: (*to TOM*) Where is spring, then? Why hasn't spring come?

BILL: I suppose, at some point –

EVELYN: At some point you have to let go.

COLETTE: Why do you want him dead?

EVELYN: What?

COLETTE: Ever since you came here, you've been reciting his eulogy. Telling me to move on. Encouraging me to go forward into the rest of my life. Grieve and then move on.

EVELYN: For your own good, Colette.

COLETTE: Not for my own good; for *your* own good. There is no rest of my life. We made a vow.

EVELYN: But if he's gone –

BILL: There's no rush.

TOM: If I'm gone, they say.

COLETTE: There's no body.

BILL: There may never be.

TOM: Evidence.

❄

JASPER: I believe people come back. Maybe not even as themselves, but in other forms.

COLETTE: (*to BILL*) Why would it just stop? We were negotiating. Why would they stop? It doesn't make sense.

TOM: There's lots that doesn't make sense.

BILL: If they still had him, they wouldn't have stopped. They would have kept negotiating. He's no use to them otherwise.

TOM: True.

COLETTE: (*to BILL*) We should have hired a professional. Why didn't we hire one of those private negotiators?

BILL: You thought you could make your own deal.

COLETTE: (*to BILL*) That's right; we thought we could make a deal. That's right.

BILL: You wanted to be close to it; you didn't want some third party to screw it up.

COLETTE: They would have screwed it up.

BILL: We did what we thought was right.

COLETTE: We sent the email. We said the money was on its way, Bill. I'm so confused, I can't remember. I can't remember sending that email. All I can see is a jumble of letters.

BILL: I sent it; I sent the email.

COLETTE: That's right.

BILL: You couldn't do it, remember? You were shaking so badly. I sent it.

COLETTE: We said, right? We said in the email.

BILL: We said the money was on its way. We did everything.

COLETTE: Did we? Two and a half weeks in Tumaco, wandering the streets? That was everything? Why did I ever let you talk me into leaving there?

BILL: We were getting in the way. We were compromising the investigation.

COLETTE: Were we? I think we were getting closer to the truth. I think we were starting to discover just how corrupt those officials were.

BILL: They asked us to leave, and we left.

COLETTE: I should have stayed.

BILL: There was nothing we could do.

BILL touches her; she impulsively draws near and then withdraws.

COLETTE: So this worked out pretty well for you, then.

BILL: Sorry?

COLETTE: The whole thing worked out pretty well for you. Tom out of the picture. You, me. Wait a year. Let her get over it.

BILL: Don't do this.

COLETTE: Let her – do her thing. Then show up one evening with a bunch of –

Suddenly, she retreats.

I'm sorry.

Beat.

Thank you for the flowers.

BILL: You don't mean any if this.

COLETTE smiles. BILL exits.

COLETTE: (*to TOM*) I do mean it. But I'll just tell him I don't, Tom. I'll tell him how sweet he is and how happy he makes me feel to at least have someone to comfort me. To look out for me. Until you come back. And when you walk through that door, what then? What will become of their condolences and bouquets and their moving on and their grieving fucking layers of fucking onion?

✳

JASPER enters; COLETTE switches gears.

COLETTE: Did you say Cartagena?

JASPER: Uh, yeah.

COLETTE: When was this?

JASPER: Back in – April, I think.

✳

COLETTE: (*to TOM*) April. He might have seen you. You might
have passed him in some narrow street, Tom. You might
have looked at one another. I know what you would have
thought of him. Instantly. You would have smiled to yourself;
he would have reminded you. That trip we did. That awful
trip. That hot, hot room. The fat, rude woman with the boy. I
couldn't move. You went for a doctor. Oh, that doctor. That
place. That was the year before we got married. I can see you
coming back with the doctor, through the bright, sunlit door.
I thought you'd never return, but you came back. It was like
a dream. I should never have doubted it. You said it. You
said, "I'll be back." But there was part of me, Tom, part of me
– shivering and shaking in that hot, airless room – that
thought you might not make good on your promise. Why
did I ever doubt you? Why did I ever, for a second, think you
would never return? What if nothing grows this year? What
if nothing comes to life? We have to ask ourselves these
questions. What if everything we hold to be true is no longer
true? Why is some forgotten outpost in Colombia of interest
to a bunch of civil engineers and geologists? Are we doing
something wrong? Are we somewhere we shouldn't be?

❄

BILL: It's development.

COLETTE: Development of what? Why would they take my
husband? If it was good for them, this development, why
would they take him? What is this development? In whose
interest is this? Not mine. I have no interest in Colombia. I
hate it there.

❄

JASPER: You know it?

COLETTE: I've been there twice: once, before we got married,
and then –

JASPER: Cartagena is pretty cool. A lot of pretty cool stuff.
Markets.

COLETTE: I don't remember any markets. I was sick in a room
the whole time, the heat.

EVELYN: Me, I am not a hot kind of person.

COLETTE: Truer words were never spoken.

They play Scrabble.

EVELYN: That's not an English word. All right, I'll give it to you,
but it's not an English word.

COLETTE: Don't just give it to me because you feel sorry for me.
Forty-eight points.

JASPER: Is "cruvix" a word?

EVELYN: No. You can make "crux." That's a word.

COLETTE: I like "cruvix." I think if it had a meaning it would be quite a good word.

JASPER: Like, a body part, maybe. Like, this is your cruvix.

He touches the inside of COLETTE's elbow.

EVELYN: Play or pass.

COLETTE: (*to TOM*) When he touches me, I feel connected to something that is somehow connected to you. Ever since he told me about Cartagena, I feel like – I know him.

TOM: You do know him.

COLETTE: (*to TOM*) But more than I should.

TOM: You're mixing a lot of things up in your mind. It's all right, but you're mixing a lot of things up.

COLETTE: (*to TOM*) Well, reality isn't really doing much for me at the moment.

EVELYN: Bill called.

COLETTE: And?

EVELYN: I think you upset him.

COLETTE: And?

JASPER: That's not good.

EVELYN: You've said something to upset him.

COLETTE: I think I've been perfectly civil.

JASPER: How come *O* is only worth one?

EVELYN: Supply and demand. Play.

COLETTE: Since when is being perfectly civil to someone
    upsetting?

EVELYN: I think he expects more than that.

JASPER: He has the hots for you, most definitely.

COLETTE: Yes, Jasper. That's quite – apparent to everyone.

JASPER: I'm only saying. Hey, I don't blame him. I mean, you're
    older and everything, but you're still pretty attractive.

COLETTE: Isn't that nice, Evelyn; I'm still pretty attractive.

EVELYN: You are.

JASPER: The light shines on you in a different way than it shines
    on anyone else.

COLETTE: Of course, I am sitting under a lamp.

❄

EVELYN: I don't like it.

COLETTE: He's harmless.

EVELYN: Well, I've seen harmless before. There's something about that boy.

COLETTE: There is.

BILL appears.

❄

BILL: Did you sleep with him?

COLETTE: I can't sleep with anybody, Bill. My husband is still alive.

BILL: You slept with him.

COLETTE: I lay down beside him. It felt comfortable. It felt right. It was the first time I've cried. Do you believe in synchronicity? I think it's no accident that he's here.

❄

COLETTE and JASPER.

JASPER: You have beautiful eyes.

COLETTE: Considering we're in the dark, I'll take it as a compliment.

JASPER: I can see in the dark.

COLETTE: Night vision.

JASPER: I don't mean just a pretty colour. I mean it's like the deepest lake, ever.

COLETTE: Oh?

JASPER: Like that lake, near Banff.

COLETTE: I don't know that lake.

JASPER: There's a lake, six hundred feet deep. Can you imagine?

COLETTE: I can't.

JASPER: That's what your eyes are like to me. Unimaginable.

❄

BILL: I found out a little something about this kid.

COLETTE: What did you find out?

BILL: I found out that when he first arrived in town, he was asking about you.

COLETTE: Why would he be doing that?

BILL: So much for synchronicity.

The spell is broken.

COLETTE: How does he know me?

BILL: Maybe you should ask him.

❄

EVELYN: How *could* he know you?

COLETTE: Maybe he read about the kidnapping in the paper.

＊

BILL: I know that you like this kid, and I don't want you to think I don't understand. I do understand. I mean, I don't really understand, but I am trying to understand. Something in you needs to be touched by something in him. Maybe it's about lost souls or longing, or I don't know.

COLETTE: You're really looking out for me, aren't you? You really care about me.

BILL: I've always cared about you. I feel – I feel like I wanted Tom to go away. I don't think I consciously thought it, but I must have, sort of, felt it. That first night, when I came over for dinner, I felt completely ashamed about what I wanted to do, but I couldn't help it. In our lives, we're told – something tells us – that there is a special person for us. What we're not told is that person might be already taken. Timing, that's the tragedy. Anyway, you're wrong about one thing. This did not turn out well for me.

COLETTE: I'm sorry I said that.

BILL: This turned out worse than I could ever have imagined. To see you alone, and –

COLETTE: I'm not alone.

BILL: The first day I saw you, in the hardware store.

COLETTE: Can I put this in my novel?

BILL: I don't mind you making fun. I know you have feelings for me.

COLETTE: It's true, Bill. You're right. (*to TOM*) Actually, it's not true but what can I tell him?

❄

EVELYN: How can you not want a man in your life?

COLETTE: I like boys better.

EVELYN: This is dangerous.

COLETTE: How?

EVELYN: He was asking for you, in town. When he first arrived. He was camped in the picnic grounds. He started a fire. And the police took him in.

COLETTE: And they let him go.

EVELYN: And he went into O'Grady's, and he was asking about you. Why?

COLETTE: There doesn't have to be a reason.

EVELYN: But there usually is.

COLETTE: He must have read about it in the paper.

EVELYN: It doesn't add up. He read about it in the paper? What paper? Where?

COLETTE: Does it matter where?

❄

JASPER: It doesn't matter.

COLETTE: (*to TOM*) Why Cartagena? Of all the places he could have mentioned he'd been.

TOM: You see? You can't help it. You're looking for connections.

COLETTE: (*to TOM*) More like the connections are looking for me.

JASPER: I'm not sure how to answer your question, Colette.

COLETTE: It's a simple enough question.

JASPER: There was a sign up at the community centre, with your name on it.

COLETTE: What sign?

JASPER: For golf clubs. It had your name and your phone number.

Beat.

COLETTE: You want to buy a set of golf clubs?

JASPER: I'd have to see them first.

❄

EVELYN: And you believe him.

COLETTE: There *is* a sign up.

EVELYN: It's the dead of winter. He's buying golf clubs in March.

COLETTE: And I'm selling them.

❄

JASPER: Don't ask me why. I can't say why.

COLETTE: You're just looking for a connection. Something to connect you to someplace, right? You see a name and number.

JASPER: That's right.

COLETTE: I get it.

JASPER: Yeah?

EVELYN: (*elsewhere*) I don't.

COLETTE: You're drifting, like snow. You want to stop drifting.

JASPER: Like snow.

COLETTE: So you drifted to me.

JASPER: That's right.

COLETTE: Maybe it is random, Tom. Maybe I have to let go. I'm so afraid. I was afraid spring would never come, and now I'm afraid it will. I'm afraid green shoots of crocuses will pop out of the cold ground. I'm afraid things will grow again, but you will never come.

JASPER reaches out his hand to her.

JASPER: He won't.

COLETTE: Why do you say it like that?

JASPER: Come with me.

COLETTE follows JASPER.

COLETTE: (*to TOM*) I'm going to let go. I don't know what else
to do. If the ice melts and everything comes back, and still
you don't come back. I ordered that Baileys, and you looked
at me, and you knew – we both knew – and you took my
hand in that moment, and you held on to my hand, and you
said, you said maybe when you came back we would try
again for a baby. I didn't tell you then; the moment wasn't
right. About the – situation. There will be no baby, Tom. I'm
not the woman I'm supposed to be, the woman you thought
you married. But the moment was never right, and I was
afraid it would – it would – I'm so cold, Tom. So cold. The
wind off the lake.

TOM: It's all right.

COLETTE: (*to TOM*) You're only saying that.

TOM: I'm not, actually. You're only imagining I am.

JASPER: Come to bed.

COLETTE: (*to TOM*) His soul. What is it about him? What is it?

TOM: He's young. He reminds you of something.

COLETTE: (*to TOM*) Cartagena. In all that heat and all that
suffering, in all that weird noise and awfulness and raging
fever – you, holding my hand. Nothing else. Just us. Then
you let go of it. "I'll be back," you said. I held on to that.

JASPER: He won't come back.

COLETTE: You seem so certain.

JASPER: I can feel things.

COLETTE: And if I squint my eyes, that hot sun pouring in
through the doorway –

JASPER: It's me. And you.

❄

COLETTE: And after we made love, Tom, I felt, for the first time
in a year; I felt – peace. Is it so terrible to finally feel that? To
feel peace? And then –

A look of horror crosses her face.

JASPER: Colette.

COLETTE: (*to TOM*) I looked over beside the bed. Just happened
to look over.

JASPER: What is it?

COLETTE: (*to TOM*) Lying there, under some of his things.

Beat.

COLETTE: (*to JASPER*) Nothing. It's nothing. (*to TOM*) Where
did he get it?

JASPER: Come to bed.

COLETTE: (*to TOM*) Where did he get your wallet, Tom? Where
on earth did he get your wallet?

Beat.

JASPER: Come back to bed.

Blackout.

ACT TWO

*As in Act One, the scenes in Act Two are fragmented,
quickly moving from one time and location to another.*

*Lights up on COLETTE and TOM. He is dressed to
leave and is holding a suitcase.*

TOM: I'll call you from Miami.

COLETTE: Is the car coming?

TOM: Five minutes.

> *Beat.*

I don't want to go.

COLETTE: Could you please not say that? Could you please not
tell me you don't want to go.

TOM: I *don't.*

COLETTE: So that I can say, "No, go," so that it can alleviate this
vague feeling of guilt you have about leaving me in the
middle of nowhere for two weeks. Tom, it's your job. Go.
There – guilt alleviated. You're welcome. Use sunscreen.

TOM: Colette, it was your idea to move out to the middle of
    nowhere, away from your friends, your family. You wanted to
    be able to write. You wanted to figure out who you were, or
    who you weren't; I can't remember. Did you ever figure that
    out? I don't even like it here.

COLETTE: Well, luckily you're never here.

TOM: You know what I particularly don't like?

COLETTE: Precambrian granite formations?

TOM: I don't like who we are here. We took ourselves out of our
    own lives. We had a nice group of friends –

COLETTE: Your friends.

TOM: Our friends.

COLETTE: But they started as your friends.

TOM: Does it make any difference? We have no social life here.

COLETTE: I'm sorry; what about the community-centre
    corn roast?

TOM: Oh, gosh. You're right, of course.

COLETTE: All right, we'll go back. I don't like it here, either.

TOM: You're just saying that.

COLETTE: Well, whether I'm saying it, or I'm just saying it, I've
    said it. We'll go back.

TOM: And we'll keep trying?

COLETTE: Tom – I need to –

TOM: We'll keep trying.

COLETTE: Yes, now go. Leave. Hurry. Get out.

TOM: You know what? I'm not going.

COLETTE: What do you mean?

TOM: I mean, I'm not going.

COLETTE: You have to go.

TOM: No, I'll call. I'll say I'm not up to speed yet. I'll stay. I'm staying.

COLETTE: Don't be ridiculous.

TOM: You said we needed to talk. Yesterday. But then we didn't talk.

COLETTE: We can talk when you get back.

TOM: And I have to carry this with me now, for two weeks. I have to *wonder* what it is that my wife wants to talk about when I get back? I'm not going.

COLETTE: All right, don't go.

Beat. He sighs.

TOM: What'll you do tonight? Do you have plans?

COLETTE: Plans?

TOM: Why don't you have Bill over?

COLETTE: Look, the lake is finally breaking up. There'll be no ice by the time you get back. Let's keep the place for the summer; we can sell it in the fall.

TOM: The car is here. I don't want to go.

COLETTE: Go.

TOM: Have a word with Mrs. God-Help-the-Lot-of-Us for me.

COLETTE: Yes.

TOM: I'll be back.

COLETTE: You'll be back.

TOM :And Colette?

COLETTE: Yes?

The mood shifts.

TOM: Find out about my wallet.

COLETTE gasps, suddenly remembering.

JASPER appears, suddenly in the room. TOM is gone, even in her imagination.

JASPER: Hey. Morning.

COLETTE: Morning. Morning.

JASPER: Was there – someone here just now?

COLETTE: No. I was talking to Evelyn.

JASPER: She's upstairs.

COLETTE: Is she?

JASPER: I guess you must be going crazy.

The joke doesn't work, so he approaches her.

COLETTE: Did you sleep well?

JASPER: You're okay about last night, right?

COLETTE: Last night. Yes, I'm … good.

JASPER: Are you? Are you? Hey. I feel like some – yeah, some
breakfast. I'm going to make you my special eggs.

He gets close.

COLETTE: What's special about them?

JASPER: I make them.

He kisses her, then stops.

This is weird.

COLETTE: I thought you never ate in the morning.

JASPER: You seem – I don't know.

COLETTE: Do I?

JASPER: I'm in Mr. McKenny's robe. Is this weird?

COLETTE: What's weird?

EVELYN appears for a moment.

EVELYN: I'll tell you what's weird.

Back to COLETTE and JASPER.

COLETTE: It looks good on you. It looks –

JASPER: You are a very – you are a very beautiful person.

COLETTE: And you, young man, are a very – young man.

JASPER: I guess I'm old enough.

EVELYN: (*as JASPER exits to the kitchen*) He isn't Tom. Just so
    you know – with or without the robe.

COLETTE: I'm aware of that.

EVELYN: What's wrong? Something's wrong. I know you.

COLETTE: Oh, Evelyn, you think you know me. You don't know
    me at all.

EVELYN: You look tired; I'm going to make you some breakfast.
    You never eat.

COLETTE: He's already making breakfast.

EVELYN: Oh.

COLETTE: Special eggs.

EVELYN: Sounds creepy.

COLETTE: Doesn't it.

EVELYN: (*suddenly realizing*) Colette! No!

COLETTE: What?

EVELYN: Colette, say you didn't have sex with him.

COLETTE: I didn't have sex with him.

EVELYN: Colette, he's a teenager. Look at me.

COLETTE: He's not a teenager.

EVELYN: I knew it. I knew this would happen. You're lonely; you're desperate. He comes here; you feel vulnerable. Something about his age makes you forget how old you really are. Before you know it –

COLETTE: Before I know it –

EVELYN: I'm going to step in here, Colette. Once again, I'm going to have to be the voice of reason.

COLETTE: Be the voice of reason.

EVELYN: You always made fun of me because I was the practical one, but it's times like this when you say to yourself, "Oh, thank goodness, Evelyn is the practical one." Yes, I am practical, and I'll tell you why – because you were always jumping off the deep end. You were always putting yourself in jeopardy. And I protected you. I have always protected you.

COLETTE: You have. Why?

EVELYN: Colette, this boy is half your age. There's a reason that people don't have relationships with people half their age. Because – they're – half – their age.

COLETTE: Is this because I'm not a complete person?

EVELYN: Don't talk about complete persons. If you want to see a person who was not a complete person, try working the emergency room.

COLETTE: I have always allowed myself to be taken over by other people, invaded, colonized. I'm like that island that nobody seems to own: sitting out there in the middle of the lake, just waiting for occupants.

(*to TOM*) She's right, Tom; she always looked out for me. And I let her. She was my conscience. My voice of reason. Then you came along, and you became my voice; without you, I don't even know who I am. You're not even here, and I still talk to you. I have no wholeness; I am, I have always been, only part.

EVELYN: Colette – pay attention.

COLETTE: (*to TOM*) I can't tell her anything; she'll go to the police. We'll scare him off.

EVELYN: We need to get rid of him. Listen to me.

COLETTE: I don't want to get rid of him. I can't.

EVELYN: We'll make up some story about having to get back to
the city.

COLETTE: I need him to stay.

EVELYN: This was exactly the kind of thing I was talking about,
letting some drifter stay here, dressing him in your
husband's clothes.

❄

JASPER enters from the kitchen.

JASPER: Let's go for a walk out on the lake today.

Beat.

COLETTE: You go.

EVELYN: We're busy.

JASPER: What are you doing?

EVELYN: We're having a discussion about something practical;
it wouldn't interest you.

JASPER: Now I know you're being funny. See, I didn't get that
about you before.

EVELYN: No?

JASPER: No.

EVELYN: The truth is, we have to go back to the city for a while.

JASPER: You do?

COLETTE: We don't. We don't, really.

EVELYN: What she means is, we do, really.

JASPER: Let me know when you make up your mind. Your breakfast is ready.

He goes.

EVELYN: I'm not eating anything he's cooked.

COLETTE: Oh God.

EVELYN: I'll do the talking. I'll explain that we have business in town.

COLETTE: Evelyn, I don't want to go away. I need to stay here; I need to figure something out.

EVELYN: What? What do you need to figure out? Are you even listening to me?

COLETTE's mind flashes to TOM for a moment.

COLETTE: (*to TOM*) You're pretty resourceful, Tom. You could have been leaving a trail. You drop the wallet; the kid picks it up. Maybe you wanted someone to pick it up. Maybe you wanted someone to find it; lead us to you. But we know what happens if the police get involved. He'll only lie to them. They'll have no choice but to let him go. They can't legally hold him. He'll run. He'll freak out, and he'll run. There's a reason he came here. Why would he come here? Maybe he's been told something. Maybe they told him to come here. Why would he come here? He was asking for me. He was asking for me in town. Tom?

EVELYN: I'll pack everything; just leave it to me. We only have to go back for a couple of days. You need some distance, anyway. You need some perspective.

COLETTE: What sort of perspective?

EVELYN: How about: you had sex with a child. And please don't tell Bill.

COLETTE: I have no intention of telling anyone anything.

BILL enters.

BILL: You seem so distant these past few days.

COLETTE: More than usual?

BILL: Yes.

COLETTE: I've got a lot on my mind.

BILL: More than usual?

COLETTE: Yes.

BILL: Can I do anything? Let me do something.

COLETTE: You can – be the wonderful neighbour that you are.

BILL: Neighbour.

COLETTE's mind flashes to TOM for a moment.

COLETTE: *(to TOM)* I need to tell him. I need to tell someone. Where are you, Tom? Why weren't you down at the tree this morning?

✳

JASPER enters, now dressed.

JASPER: Hey. You know what I read once?

Beat.

COLETTE: No.

JASPER: I read that Jesus walked on water, right, because it was frozen. Get it? That's how he walked on it. They thought it was a miracle, but it was just that the sea froze over. They were all, like, hey, he's walking on water.

COLETTE: That – Jesus.

JASPER: Yeah, I read that.

COLETTE: Who knows what to believe anymore?

JASPER: Yeah. Who knows?

He goes.

EVELYN: I'm absolutely terrible at pretending that nothing's happened.

COLETTE: Nobody's asking you to pretend anything. Nothing's happened.

EVELYN: I have too much integrity for this.

COLETTE: Oh, please.

EVELYN: You think I don't have integrity?

COLETTE: I don't know what to think.

JASPER passes through.

JASPER: Do I look too much like your husband in this parka?

EVELYN: Yes.

COLETTE: No.

JASPER: You all right?

COLETTE: Weren't you going out?

JASPER: I want you to come with me.

COLETTE: I've – got some things I have to do here.

EVELYN: Excuse me. I have a – have a –

EVELYN exits.

JASPER: What's with her?

COLETTE: She's just being odd.

JASPER: Something's wrong.

COLETTE: Women – our age – sometimes – get odd.

JASPER: She's related to you; that's funny.

COLETTE: Why?

JASPER: Related to you, but can't relate to you.

COLETTE: Oh, a play on words.

JASPER: Come here.

COLETTE: I'm –

JASPER takes COLETTE in his arms and holds her.

JASPER: We can relate.

He smiles; she returns the smile.

COLETTE: We can.

JASPER: Are you really going back into town?

COLETTE: What if I did?

JASPER: I'd wait for you.

They kiss. Beat. He releases her and exits.

COLETTE: (*to TOM*) Oh, Tom. I trusted him; I even fell a little bit in love with him. You must forgive me. What I did. And now I'm being punished for losing my faith. Where are you? I went down to the tree this morning. You weren't there. I shouldn't have slept with him. There is a right and a wrong in this world, and I am being punished. I should have known you were alive. I should never have stopped believing it. I gave up on you. I threw it all away in a moment of –

EVELYN appears.

EVELYN: I've had an idea. We book a cruise. We cruise the
    Caribbean for a couple of weeks.

COLETTE: I'm not going anywhere.

EVELYN: What is it about intercourse?

COLETTE: Must you call it "intercourse"?

EVELYN: Well, what else is it called?

COLETTE: You've been watching too many documentaries.

EVELYN: What is it about *sexual relations* that makes people
    think it's some kind of solution? To me it's the beginning of
    problems, not the end. It's incredibly complicated, not to
    mention the whole procreation thing.

COLETTE: He was wearing a condom.

EVELYN: This is all very graphic; thank you.

COLETTE: You're a nurse, for God's sake.

EVELYN: Exactly.

COLETTE: And, anyway, I can't get pregnant.

EVELYN: What are you talking about?

COLETTE: I can't get pregnant.

EVELYN: When – did we find this out?

COLETTE: I've known for a long time. In Colombia, when I had
    the appendectomy, there was an infection.

EVELYN: You should have come home.

COLETTE: I couldn't, and, anyway, it could have happened here.

EVELYN: It would never have happened here.

COLETTE: All right, it would never have happened here, but I couldn't get home, and so it happened there.

EVELYN: He never said anything to me.

COLETTE: Who?

EVELYN: Tom.

COLETTE: Why would he say anything to you?

EVELYN: It's true. He didn't like me.

COLETTE: *Doesn't* like you.

EVELYN: Really?

COLETTE: And, anyway, he didn't know. I didn't know myself for the longest time.

EVELYN: You didn't tell him?

COLETTE: He didn't ask.

EVELYN: He didn't –

COLETTE: I was – getting there. I was – getting around to it. The morning he left – oh, Evelyn, let's not talk about this.

EVELYN: I can't believe you never told anyone.

COLETTE: There are many couples who don't have children. He
would have – eventually, he would have –

✳

(to TOM) I was afraid you would leave me, Tom. I was afraid
of my incompleteness. I could see in your eyes, the intent.
The hope. Every time we made love, I could feel your
hopefulness, and it burned in me, until it burned away all
my happiness and reason for being.

✳

EVELYN: You think he wouldn't have understood?

COLETTE: My imaginary Tom, maybe.

EVELYN: Your what?

COLETTE: (to TOM) Under the tree. Two summers ago. I think it
was late June or early July; I'm pretty sure it was, because the
lake was still really clear. You could see almost to the
bottom – one of those days. I went up to get you a beer. When
I came back, you were asleep. I watched you breathing long,
easy breaths. I thought about our lives together. By then I
knew about the affair, or suspected. But it was like the truth
was somewhere else, up at the house – it didn't matter. Down
here, by the water, under the tree, it was all gone; just us. You
woke up suddenly, and you looked over at me and squinted.
You smiled. That was it. Before anybody spoke. Before
anybody thought. Before another second passed and time
moved on again, dragging everything with it – love.
All-forgiving, all-knowing love. It wasn't really even a smile.

EVELYN: If you love a person –

COLETTE: It doesn't always work like that, Evelyn. Sometimes all that keeps us going is the potential for something more.

EVELYN: Who needs children?

COLETTE: Well, the species, but aside from that –

EVELYN: Species?

Beat.

Oh. The species.

COLETTE: We see the future through them. Without the future, the present has no meaning.

EVELYN: Don't talk to me about the future; at least you have someone missing in your life; I don't even have that. I'm sorry; what a weird thing to say.

❄

BILL: I believe the present has meaning.

EVELYN: It's about the only thing that does.

BILL: Where did they go?

EVELYN: For another walk around the lake.

BILL: Another walk around the lake.

EVELYN: I wouldn't suspect anything.

BILL: No?

EVELYN: Sometimes I think you and I are the only two people
around here – who – have – any sense of – who have any
sense.

BILL: I don't have any sense at all. Can I tell you a secret, Evelyn?

EVELYN: You can tell me anything.

BILL: I haven't told anyone.

EVELYN: That's pretty much the definition of a secret.

BILL: I'm in love with Colette.

EVELYN: That's – not a secret.

BILL: I feel as if I've done something wrong.

EVELYN: How?

BILL: I don't want him to come back. It's horrible, but it's what I
feel. You think what's in your heart is good, but then –

EVELYN: We can't be blamed for the bad that happens in this
world. Sometimes we even take advantage of it.

BILL: Isn't that awfully cold?

EVELYN: There's cold all around us.

As BILL considers this.

❄

JASPER and COLETTE are out on the lake;
COLETTE's focus is again split.

COLETTE: (*to JASPER*) I don't think spring will ever come.

JASPER: I believe it already has.

COLETTE: (*to TOM*) What does he want, Tom? Why won't he just tell me?

JASPER: Why don't you look at me?

COLETTE: (*to TOM*) I have to not act differently. I have to pretend nothing's wrong.

JASPER: Is something wrong?

COLETTE: (*to TOM*) It's like he's inside my head.

JASPER: You're wondering about me. You're wondering why I came here. You're always wondering why I came here.

COLETTE: You came for the golf clubs, which, by the way, you haven't even looked at.

JASPER: I didn't come for the golf clubs.

COLETTE: No?

JASPER: You know that.

COLETTE: Do I?

JASPER: I came to see who you were.

COLETTE: Who am I?

JASPER: I see a sign posted outside a grocery store. I ask myself, "Why is this person named Colette selling a set of men's golf clubs in the dead of winter?"

COLETTE: Is that true?

JASPER: Why not?

COLETTE: What else is true?

JASPER: For instance?

COLETTE: Why are you here?

JASPER: Can't I just be here? Does there have to be a reason?

COLETTE: Sure, we can all be here. There doesn't have to be a reason. It could all just be random – all of it – but there's always some crazy logic.

JASPER: You think I'm crazy?

COLETTE: I think we're all crazy. Tell me about Cartagena.

JASPER: What about it?

COLETTE: What was it like?

JASPER: You've been there.

COLETTE: That was a while ago. Places change. I was very sick.

JASPER: I think I told you; I was with a girl.

COLETTE: A Dutch girl. She ran off with some Americans.

JASPER: Was she Dutch?

COLETTE: You said she was Dutch, with a tattoo on the back of her hand.

JASPER: How come you remember things like that? They're not important.

COLETTE: Aren't they?

JASPER: Let's go make love.

COLETTE: Jasper, I think maybe I made a mistake. I think I might have rushed things.

JASPER: How?

COLETTE: Well, I don't – *know* you. A person should know a person.

JASPER: You know me.

COLETTE: I don't. There's so much about you I don't know. For instance, is Jasper your real name?

 Beat.

JASPER: Why? Did somebody tell you something?

COLETTE: It's just that, as names go –

JASPER: Maybe it's where I'm headed. Who knows, right? You know what a name is; it's an identity. If you have the same name your whole life, it means you're always the same person.

COLETTE: That's – sort of the idea.

JASPER: My identity is about where I'm headed.

❄

EVELYN: Maybe he should call himself "Nowhere."

BILL: Or "Prison."

❄

COLETTE: (to JASPER) I thought you were headed for Thunder Bay?

JASPER: Why all this information? What's it got to do with anything? It's just you and me. Just you, and just me.

COLETTE: Is it?

JASPER: You've gone all different. You've gone all cold. I knew this would happen.

COLETTE: (to TOM) It's not working. He senses how close I am. He's going to run.

JASPER: Maybe I need to get lost for a while.

COLETTE: (to JASPER) You are lost. Maybe you need to stay.

JASPER: For how long before you change your mind?

COLETTE: About what?

❄

EVELYN: How was your walk?

JASPER: Cold.

EVELYN: Did she explain to you that we have to go back to the city for a bit? She's reluctant to talk about it because, well, she knows it means you'll have to head on out of here, and she has a great fondness for you; although it's a mixture, I would have to say, of fondness, confusion, and grief.

JASPER: Or I'll stay.

EVELYN: Where?

JASPER: Maybe I'll look after the place while you're gone.

EVELYN: Bill does that.

JASPER: I heard you talking yesterday, to Colette.

EVELYN: We talk all the time.

JASPER: About me.

EVELYN: We talk all the time about you.

JASPER: And what do you say?

EVELYN: Say? We say that you're – interesting. An interesting person.

JASPER: Interesting in what way?

EVELYN: In – no way.

JASPER: You think I've done something wrong.

EVELYN: I wouldn't know.

JASPER: I haven't done anything wrong.

EVELYN: Well, I'm relieved. It's good to know when somebody hasn't done anything wrong.

JASPER: Maybe it's *you* that's done something wrong.

EVELYN: Such as?

JASPER: I am who I am.

EVELYN: That's reassuring.

JASPER: Is it so wrong to care about somebody?

EVELYN: You care about somebody?

JASPER: Colette.

EVELYN: Oh, Colette.

JASPER: Why don't you like me?

EVELYN: I never said that. Did I say that?

JASPER: Ever since yesterday, you've been acting kind of unfriendly towards me.

EVELYN: Only since yesterday?

    JASPER moves in.

You're standing awfully close.

JASPER: Am I?

EVELYN: What are you doing here?

JASPER: What am I doing here? I belong here. Do you belong
here? I don't like people questioning my motives.

EVELYN: You have motives?

❄

COLETTE *appears.*

COLETTE: (*to EVELYN*) Why did you say anything?

EVELYN: I didn't say anything.

❄

JASPER: I think I have to leave tomorrow.

COLETTE: No. No, you don't.

JASPER: People don't like me here. There's not a lot of trust
around here.

COLETTE: I like you.

JASPER: She doesn't know what's going on.

COLETTE: No? What's going on?

❄

BILL: Why don't you come right out and ask him?

COLETTE: He'll run. We can't let him go.

BILL: Then call the police.

COLETTE: (*to TOM*) I told Bill. I had to tell someone.

BILL: I'm glad you did.

COLETTE: (*to TOM*) But I didn't tell him everything. I told him about the wallet, but I didn't tell him everything.

BILL: You're not a detective, Colette. He could be dangerous. You're not the police.

COLETTE: If there's a connection, I need to make it. I need answers. I promised Tom.

BILL: Tom?

✳

JASPER: Huh?

COLETTE: Just – talk to me.

JASPER: I want somebody to have some faith in me for a change.

COLETTE: All right, tell me about Tumaco.

JASPER: Hey?

COLETTE: Tumaco, it's a town in southern Colombia. Weren't you in Tumaco?

JASPER: Did I say that?

COLETTE: I don't know. I thought you said that.

JASPER: Yeah, the surf is really great there.

COLETTE: You surf?

JASPER: Are you getting sexy with me?

COLETTE: You never told me you surfed.

JASPER: It's all part of the mystery.

COLETTE: The mystery of Jasper.

JASPER: That's right.

COLETTE: Come to think of it, you hadn't actually told me
you'd been to Tumaco. But now, it seems, you have.

> *Beat.*

It's where my husband disappeared.

> *Beat.*

JASPER: Right.

COLETTE: I've never met anyone who's been there.

JASPER: Now you have.

COLETTE: Now I have.

JASPER: You want this all to make sense.

COLETTE: It will make sense.

JASPER: What if it doesn't, Colette? What if nothing makes any sense?

COLETTE: Nobody's even heard of the place, that I know of.

BILL: The kid keeps changing his story.

COLETTE: He just keeps telling more of it.

BILL: I think you should call the police.

COLETTE: Let me do this my way.

EVELYN enters for a moment.

EVELYN: You look so stressed.

COLETTE: (*to TOM*) They want me to be stressed. They want me to be exhausted from my grief, so that I can live in the same world they do, a world of giving up hope and sitting out weather. But this, this, Tom, is giving me new life. He knows something, and it's giving me my life again; a direction I can go.

BILL: You want a direction you can go? Go to the police.

COLETTE: (*to TOM*) The ice is breaking off from the eaves and crashing in great chunks onto the ground in front of the window. The ice fisherman is packing up to go.

BILL: Well, you better act soon, then, because it looks to me like he's leaving.

COLETTE: Who?

BILL: Jasper.

COLETTE: He's not going anywhere.

BILL: Then why did he ask me for a ride up the highway?

❄

COLETTE: Was it something I said?

JASPER: Yeah, it was something you said. All this talk – this talk, about Tumaco and whatever. Forget it. It's just time to move on, that's all.

COLETTE: You don't want to talk about it?

JASPER: No, I don't want to talk. All we ever do is talk.

COLETTE: All right, we'll stop talking.

JASPER: I think you're going to have my baby.

COLETTE: What?

JASPER: We slept together, and I think you're going to have my baby.

COLETTE: You wore a condom.

JASPER: Actually, no. I didn't.

Beat.

COLETTE: You said you did.

JASPER: I said I did. I didn't.

COLETTE: That's – not very responsible of you.

JASPER: Oh, and was it very responsible of you to make love to me when you don't even know my real name and when you didn't even trust me?

COLETTE: What is your real name?

JASPER: Does it make any difference now?

COLETTE: I can't have a baby. It's impossible.

JASPER: I say you can.

COLETTE: I had a terrible illness a few years ago, and it made me – unable to have children.

JASPER: Well, I say that's wrong.

COLETTE: Well, it's not wrong. Why do you want me to have a baby?

JASPER: I don't want you to have one, but I think you're going to have one. And I don't want you to get rid of it, either; I want you to keep it. You need a life that goes on, after your husband.

COLETTE: There is no "after."

She grabs him.

JASPER: Hey, let go.

COLETTE: What is happening?

JASPER: I told you. I'm going.

COLETTE: Jasper. My husband.

JASPER: Your husband, your husband. Yeah. Why did he leave you?

COLETTE: He didn't leave me. He went away on business.

JASPER: And now he's gone forever. Why would he do that?

COLETTE: He's alive. You've seen him, and he's alive.

JASPER: I haven't seen him. Why would I see him? I don't know your husband. I don't know anything about him.

COLETTE: Let me tell you, then. He's a civil engineer. He works on the petroleum pipelines. In Tumaco, there's a pipeline terminus. Tumaco is a port, okay, a port. And aside from "really great surfing," it's also a place of really great upheaval and turmoil. There are renegades and drug lords and bandits and liars and thieves. Oh, and revolutionary soldiers who say they are fighting in the name of the people – we'll have to take their word for it. But sometimes they kidnap people there for money.

JASPER: I know all this. You told me.

COLETTE: You knew all this before I told you. You knew all this in April, when you were in Tumaco. You knew all this when you arrived here, looking for me. You've known this the whole time.

JASPER: I don't know anything. I don't know anything.

COLETTE: Look at me. You know something.

JASPER: What do I know?

COLETTE: The truth.

❋

BILL: At first I wanted him never to return. I actually thought
that. I actually – But when I saw what it meant to her, how it
destroyed her so completely, I realized: the woman that I was
in love with was the woman who was Tom's wife. The
conflicted, flirtatious wife of somebody who both loved and
hated her husband. The woman who was alive. But it killed
her inside; this killed her.

EVELYN: Could you ever love anybody else as much?

BILL: I think we're all destined for loneliness.

EVELYN: What about loneliness in the company of others?

BILL: That's it, isn't it? Like trees, rooted to the spot, looking at
one another. Rooted in the ground, unable to move closer.
Trying with all our might to grow closer, our branches
reaching. But only able to imagine closeness, never touching
and growing older.

EVELYN: That is so beautiful, what you just said.

BILL: What did I say? I wasn't paying any attention. Even *I'm* not
interested in me.

❋

COLETTE: (*to TOM*) And what if he tells me you're alive, Tom?
What if he tells me you're alive? What then? You come back,
what then? We look into one another's eyes. We thank God,

or whomever, for your safe return. We go back to living? Back into life? This time of waiting, this time of waiting is so many things. Things unknown. What if I didn't love you anymore? How long would it take after your return? A week? A year? Two years, before it disintegrated finally, once and for all, childless, miserable, unfaithful. What if I love you only in your absence? What if this longing, this suffering, is all I love? Your return? What if your return brings an end, and your never returning is all that keeps it going? Tom, Tom!

JASPER: What do you want from me?

COLETTE: I need to know the truth.

JASPER: About what?

COLETTE: My husband.

> *Beat.*

JASPER: I don't know about your husband.

COLETTE: Why do you have his wallet?

JASPER: His wallet?

COLETTE: Yes, his wallet. Why do you have it?

> *JASPER is taken aback. BILL appears for a moment, elsewhere.*

BILL: The kid's a liar; don't believe a word he says.

JASPER: I found it.

COLETTE: Where?

JASPER: I found it; that's all. Is it so important?

COLETTE: Of course it's important. It's important to me! My
husband is missing. If you have his wallet, you know where
he is, Jasper.

JASPER: Where he is, is where he is.

COLETTE: Who *are* you?

JASPER: You don't know me. You fell in love with me and you
don't know me.

COLETTE: I didn't fall in love with you.

JASPER: You said you did.

COLETTE: The girl who serves drinks at O'Grady's, she has a
tattoo of a hummingbird on the back of her hand.

> *Beat.*

JASPER: Is that right?

COLETTE: Where did you get the wallet? Where did you get it?
Tell me, Jasper, so help me God, or I'll rip your fucking eyes out.

JASPER: Outside Tumaco –

> *Beat.*

– near the beach.

The ground beneath COLETTE begins to shift.

COLETTE: (*to TOM*) Oh my God, Tom. What is he saying? What
   beach? Is that where you've gone? Is that why you weren't
   under the tree this morning?

JASPER: The surfing beach.

COLETTE: (*to JASPER*) The wallet was there, on the beach?
   The wallet was just lying there?

JASPER: No. Hidden, in some tall grass, back behind the beach,
   up a little ways. There's a bunch of trees and some grass. I
   spent the night sleeping on the beach; I walked up into the
   tall grass in the morning to take a piss. There's a parking lot
   farther up. I went in there. I saw it.

COLETTE: You saw the wallet?

JASPER: The body. I saw the body.

   *Beat. She backs away. As the scene continues
   COLETTE finds herself divided between two
   realities.*

TOM: Don't be afraid.

COLETTE: (*to TOM*) There you are. Where did you go?

TOM: I told you. Tumaco.

JASPER: It was lying there. Covered over a little with some
   cardboard thing. First, I saw a leg. Then I pulled over the
   cardboard, and I kind of looked underneath, and I saw the
   whole thing, like, the whole body.

TOM: I told you I'd be back.

COLETTE: No matter what I know of myself, Tom, I couldn't have known this moment. I've stopped hearing what he's saying. I only hear birds.

JASPER: Bunch of crows, I chased them away from the body.

COLETTE: Where am I? It's just the way he described it. Near a beach. Off a little way into the grass. I can see you lying there; it's true.

JASPER: He looked pretty – beaten up.

COLETTE: Your eyes. Are they open?

JASPER: The eyes were wide open.

COLETTE: I reach down to you.

JASPER: I bent down and I looked right in the face.

COLETTE: Oh, Tom.

JASPER: The jaw was all over to one side. Blood, dried, kind of, just a fucked-up scenario. Flies all over.

COLETTE: What have they done to my husband; what have they done to this beautiful man?

JASPER: It looked pretty – you know – messed up. Like a dead animal of some kind.

COLETTE: It's all that's left; they've taken the rest.

JASPER: I reached in, and I – took his wallet.

COLETTE: Gone. Your smile, your sweet voice in my ear, your breath, your breath on me, on the back of my neck. Your impatience, your lies, your love, all gone.

TOM: So that's it.

COLETTE: Take my hand, Tom.

JASPER: I grabbed it, and I ran.

COLETTE: Let's go home.

TOM: It's good you know now. Spring is coming.

COLETTE: I feel it.

JASPER: I didn't mean to hurt anyone. I was going to give it back to you. I was going to ... give it to you. You've been so kind to me.

COLETTE's attention shifts to JASPER.

COLETTE: (*to JASPER*) Why did you come?

JASPER: I told you. I had to.

COLETTE: You had to?

JASPER: After I had the wallet for a few days, I was going to hand it in, you know, just leave it at the police station, but I just thought – I don't know. I was thinking about him, and his life with you – I – and I kept looking at your picture – in the wallet.

COLETTE: My picture.

TOM: I never told you, did I? About that picture.

JASPER: I said to myself, "I am holding a picture of this woman; I am holding her picture; I need to give it back." And the note on the other side.

COLETTE: Note?

JASPER: "Without you I am nothing," you wrote. Nothing.

COLETTE: (*to TOM*) I never wrote that.

TOM: I did.

❄

JASPER: We're something, Colette. We're not nothing.

COLETTE: (*to JASPER*) Why did you take so long?

JASPER: The summer, the fall, I just –

COLETTE: (*to TOM*) He moves about like some sort of wounded animal. I don't know who he is. He's crazy, but I don't think he's insane.

JASPER: People don't die.

COLETTE: You came here to tell me all this? Why did you come here?

JASPER: I came here; the rest, I don't know.

COLETTE: (*to TOM*) Do you believe in synchronicity, Tom?

TOM: I believe things happen.

COLETTE: For which there are reasons.

JASPER: I should go.

TOM: Reasons inside of no reasons. Constellations gather in heavenly clusters, but why? We assign perfect logic to molecules.

COLETTE: Even molecules have reasons.

TOM: Find my body. Bury me.

COLETTE: (*to TOM*) Yes.

TOM: Look, the ice is melting on the lake. We can spend the summer and in the fall –

❄

COLETTE: You need to talk to the police, Jasper. You need to tell them everything, so they can notify the Colombian authorities.

JASPER: They'll arrest me.

COLETTE: I won't let them.

JASPER: I thought I could stay here. But I was wrong. I thought I could – be with you. And you wouldn't be sad anymore. And I wouldn't be sad. And everything would be all right, and nothing would be wrong, ever.   .

COLETTE: It doesn't work like that.

JASPER: There should be no sadness; there should be no death.

COLETTE: We need to talk to the police.

※

BILL: So why didn't you call them?

COLETTE: I did, but by the time I turned around, he was gone.

EVELYN: You did what you could, Bill.

BILL: I did what I could.

EVELYN: He couldn't get near. You couldn't get near. I saw the whole thing. The ice just kept cracking.

BILL: He thought he could run away across the lake.

COLETTE: But spring is here.

BILL: I pushed a ladder along the surface, but he couldn't grab on to it.

EVELYN: I held on to Bill's feet, and he tried to grab on to Jasper.

BILL: The water was just too cold. He couldn't get a good grip. His backpack, everything.

EVELYN: You didn't want to get pulled in. Poor Bill.

BILL: He would have pulled me in.

COLETTE: The frozen lake has finally given in. Winter can only hold on to us for so long.

EVELYN: Poor, stupid kid.

COLETTE: Not stupid.

EVELYN: I didn't mean stupid, I meant – I don't know what I meant.

✳

COLETTE: I thought I knew you, but I didn't; for one moment, I thought I knew.

JASPER: What's to know about nothing? I just ended up in the world. For a while, I was looking for my family, but I gave up looking; found some other people. But they left me, too. Whenever I find people, they leave. I hope you don't mind me telling you all this. I never told anybody this. I never had anybody to tell.

COLETTE: What's it like, floating under the ice?

JASPER: Fucking cold, man.

✳

EVELYN: Who are you talking to?

COLETTE: Huh?

EVELYN: Didn't you say –? I thought you said you couldn't have a child.

COLETTE: I couldn't.

EVELYN: How depressing. I'm sorry; I didn't mean *depressing*. You're not going to have it, are you? Poor Colette. As if losing a husband isn't enough. When does the body come home?

COLETTE: He has a stopover in Miami. Isn't that funny, a stopover. Bill's going down. Bill wants to do everything. Good old Bill.

BILL: I want to help you. I want to be there for you. You have a child coming. Will you let me look after it with you?

❄

COLETTE: (*to TOM*) What can I tell him, Tom?

TOM: Tell him yes.

COLETTE: When I really mean no?

TOM: You might come to it, in time. You might come to love him.

COLETTE: The way spring comes? As if it never will; then one day, out of sheer exasperation, just – does.

BILL: I'll make you happy.

COLETTE smiles at BILL, but her attention is with TOM.

COLETTE: (*to TOM*) He won't make me happy, but I'll tell him that I am. I'll smile, and I'll bring flowers in from the garden, and I'll leave him sleeping in bed at night, to come downstairs and wander into and out of rooms, just to feel how empty they are without you in them.

❄

EVELYN: If only you knew how lucky you were.

COLETTE: (*to TOM*) That's a funny thing to say. The day we finally buried you, Tom, she said I was lucky; that I should find love so

113

soon after I lost it. And a child inside me, what an odd sensation. To feel this little life growing inside of my lifeless one.

❄

BILL: Still, I don't know if I tried hard enough to save that kid.

EVELYN: Whether you did or not.

BILL: Do you think I tried hard enough?

EVELYN: You did what you could.

BILL: I don't know; I think – sometimes I think – the things we do, without knowing.

EVELYN: All the things.

BILL: I saw in his eyes – the look in his eyes. I don't think he wanted to be saved.

EVELYN: No.

BILL: But was there something deep inside of me, too. Some wish that he – that he would – that I would –

EVELYN: You could only hold on for so long.

BILL: Not long enough.

EVELYN: It was out of our hands, Bill.

BILL: It was out of our hands, but –

EVELYN: It was always out of our hands.

EVELYN moves close to him.

BILL: I have to – I have to go.

> *EVELYN almost touches BILL; he walks away,*
> *leaving her alone.*

❄

COLETTE: Poor Evelyn.

EVELYN: I thought I should pack my things, so I packed them.
Poor Colette. I hope you'll be all right without me.

> *EVELYN exits.*

❄

COLETTE: And now that it's gone, what can we say of this
godless winter, Tom? It's left us, but not for long.

TOM: That's a pessimistic view.

COLETTE: True. Is it?

TOM: Don't you find it reassuring? Things go, but never
really go.

COLETTE: You mean Evelyn isn't really going?

TOM: I mean love exists, when everything else is long gone.

COLETTE: How was your flight home?

TOM: Uneventful.

COLETTE: Cargo isn't really the best way to fly, is it?

TOM: I'm back. That's all that matters. Now I can go.

COLETTE: You're leaving?

TOM: Well, I can't sit under that tree forever.

COLETTE: Should I come with you?

TOM: Come with me?

COLETTE: Should I?

TOM: Not for now.

TOM touches her. He goes.

COLETTE: (*to TOM*) Not for now, no. I'll wait through all these living seasons. When things blossom again, I'll know. When life returns, I'll always know. The warmth of the sun is not forever; there's another cold wind coming. And with it my heart will have to thaw, and grow warm again.

Blackout.